Still Waters of the Air

drawings by
ARVIS STEWART

The Dial Press
New York

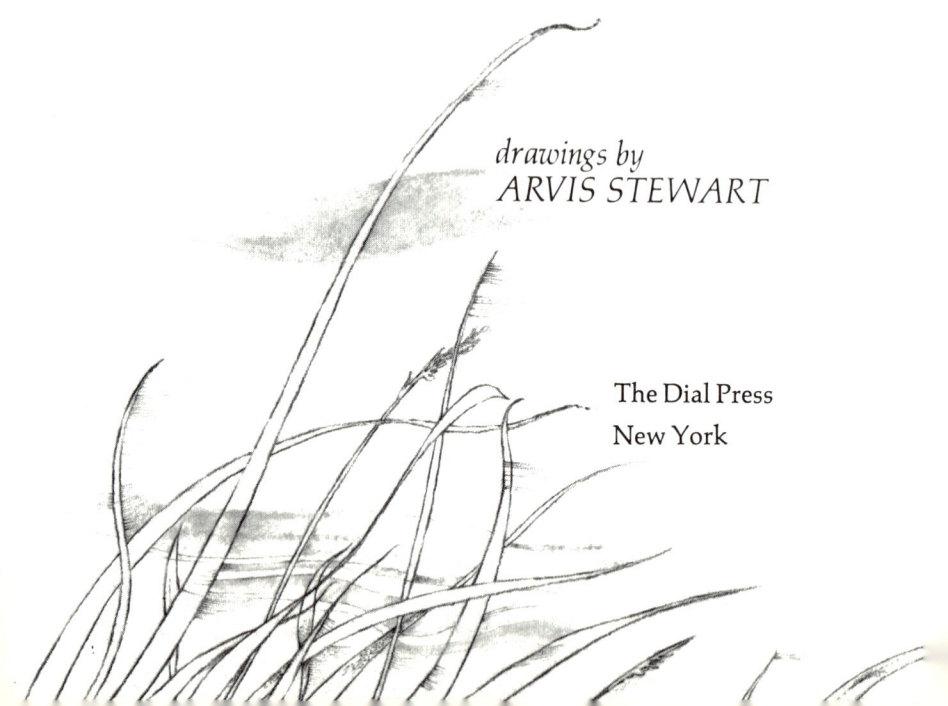

Still Waters of the Air

POEMS BY THREE MODERN SPANISH POETS

edited by
RICHARD LEWIS

ACKNOWLEDGMENTS

"Silly Song," translated by Harriet de Onis; "Snail," translated by William Jay Smith; "The Little Mute Boy," translated by W.S. Merwin; "The Lizard Is Crying," translated by Stephen Spender and J.L. Gili; "Pause of the Clock," translated by Stanley Reed; "Casida of the Golden Girl," translated by W.S. Merwin; "Balcony," translated by W.S. Merwin; "Variations," translated by Lysander Kemp; "Half Moon," translated by W.S. Merwin; "The Interrupted Concert," translated by W.S. Merwin; "Farewell," translated by W.S. Merwin: from Frederico García Lorca, SELECTED POEMS. Copyright 1955 by New Directions. Reprinted by permission of New Directions Publishing Corporation.

"My Apple Tree/Huerto de Marzo," "Down the mountain my husband . . ./Por el monte ya llega . . . ," "August/Agosto," and "In the morning unfolding . . ./Cuando se abre en la mañana . . .": from Edwin Honig, GARCÍA LORCA. Copyright 1944 by New Directions. Reprinted by permission of New Directions Publishing Corporation.

"The Weeping," translated by Kenneth Rexroth (from "Casida del Llanto" by Frederico García Lorca): Copyright © 1969 by Kenneth Rexroth. Reprinted from THIRTY SPANISH POEMS OF LOVE AND EXILE by Kenneth Rexroth by permission of City Lights Books.

"Canción Tonta," "Caracola," "El Niño Mudo," "El Lagarto Está Llorando . . . ," "Huerto de Marzo," "Claro de Reloj," "Agosto," "Casida de la Muchacha Dorada," "Balcón," "Variación," "Por el monte ya llega . . . ," "Casida del Llanto," "Media Luna," "El Concierto Interrumpido," "Cuando se abre en la mañana . . . ," and "Despedida": from Frederico García Lorca, OBRAS COMPLETAS. © Aguilar S.A. de Ediciones. All Rights Reserved. Reprinted by permission of New Directions Publishing Corporation, Agents for the Estate of Frederico García Lorca.

Quotation from THE GYPSY BALLADS OF GARCÍA LORCA on page 11, translated by Rolfe Humphreys, used by permission of Indiana University Press.

"New Leaves," "With the Roses," "Yellow Spring," "I am like a distracted child . . . ," "Light and Water," "Don't run, go slowly . . . ," "The Afternoon Roads," "Winter Song," "Sleep is

Note: The English translations in this book are for the
most part free and attempt above all to capture the spirit
of the Spanish.

R.L.

Behind the poem is the human being—a person with an attitude toward himself and the world around him. The shaping of his attitude is influenced not only by his own experiences but by the folkways and traditions of his country.

It is the poet who, in many instances, is consciously concerned with preserving the traditions of his environment or, if not with preserving, at least with understanding them. He is attuned to seeking out the cause and effect of particular patterns of thought; he brings a significance to concepts which are accepted as commonplace; he clarifies the conflict of feelings around him. He does these things, aware that as a human being and poet he must not lose sight of the past if he is to understand and speak of the present.

The three poets represented here were all born in Spain. They have built their vision, attitudes, and poetic style from the particular traditions and spirit of their country. They have opened themselves up to everything that is Spain and have absorbed every aspect of life within their land. Yet what they write about, although it is at the heart of Spanish thought and feeling, is essentially the human experience familiar to us all. The drama they portray is the universal drama of birth, life, and death that is a part of all cultures. What gives the work of these poets a particular sense of place is their ability to re-enact this drama against the landscape they know best—the harsh and beautiful Spanish landscape. It is the marriage between human experience and nature that has suggested the format of this book. Inseparable from the progression of the seasons, which change from spring, through summer and fall to winter, is the growth of man as he moves from childhood to old age and death. It is hoped that the reader will read these poems as part of the natural flow of life, sharing with the poets the road that is traveled from life to death, and listening, as they have listened to a child's dreams, caught in the onrush of spring with its flowering brambles, silver poplars, and yellow flowers. A child's dreams of snails, lizards, and his own apple tree ending in the sadness of a childhood that must be left behind, and, like the magic of light and water, vanishing "among the misty vapors, among the misty clouds." As he watches the sun bring summer to all its fullness, love and desire take hold of the man who once was a child. And in the richness of fulfillment, the summer with its harvest, a man with his beloved, suddenly death makes someone cry out: "Lord, what I most loved you tore from me./ Hear again this heart cry out alone." Autumn strips the branches, winter brings "the thud of sad snow," "a solitary poplar," "the sobbing of the tall black pines," night, sleep, and a man's farewell, dreaming, as if a child again, of life lived and still living:

And I shall go away; and be alone, homeless, with no
Green tree, with no white well,
With no blue and peaceful sky,
And the birds will still be there, singing.

Each of these poets seems to speak to the others. All

of them transmit their love of the sensuous, their fascination with the interlocking worlds of dream and reality, their probing of the mystery of death. Each gives us impressions, insights, and feelings of the land from which he draws his inspiration. And like their land, in which water, greenness, and flowers project against a landscape of arid earth, their poems, well-wrought and finely made, stand out as expressions of the human condition. They sing, as the Spanish people have always sung when they are filled with feeling—and their song echoes beyond the borders of their land. It echoes into a realm where we may all listen—and understand.

R.L.
October 1969

Federico was speaking,
flirting with death. She was listening.
"Because yesterday in my verse, friend,
the clap of your dry palms sounded,
and you gave ice to my song, and to my tragedy the
edge of your silvery sickle,
I shall sing of the flesh that you lack,
and eyes you do not have,
of your hair that the wind would toss,
and your red lips where once you were kissed . . ."

ANTONIO MACHADO
(from *The Crime Was in Granada*)

The poem should be like a star which is a world and
looks like a diamond.

JUAN RAMÓN JIMÉNEZ

The metaphor links two antagonistic worlds through an
equestrian leap of imagination . . .

FEDERICO GARCÍA LORCA

LA PRIMAVERA HA VENIDO

La primavera ha venido.
¡Aleluyas blancas
de los zarzales floridos!

ANTONIO MACHADO

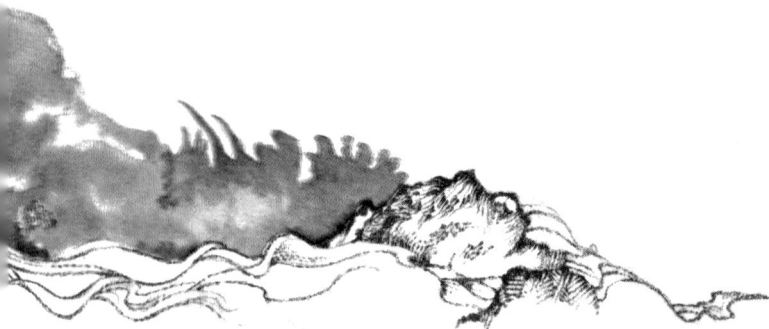

LA PRIMAVERA HA VENIDO

La primavera ha venido.
Nadie sabe cómo ha sido.

ANTONIO MACHADO

THE SPRING HAS COME

The spring has come.
White hallelujahs
of flowering brambles!

ANTONIO MACHADO

SPRING HAS COME

Spring has come.
No one knows how.

ANTONIO MACHADO

15

HOJAS NUEVAS
A Isoldita Esplá

¡Mira, por los chopos
de plata, cómo trepan al cielo niños de oro!

Y van mirando al cielo,
y suben, los ojos en el azul, cual puros sueños.

¡Mira, por los chopos
de plata, cómo trepan al cielo niños de oro!

Y el azul de sus bellos
ojos y el cielo se tocan . . . ¡Son uno ojos y cielo!

¡Mira, por los chopos
de plata, cómo trepan al cielo niños de oro!

JUAN RAMÓN JIMÉNEZ

NEW LEAVES
To Isoldita Esplá

Look how the golden children
are climbing the silver poplars to the sky!

And they go, staring at the sky,
as they climb in the blue, their eyes like pure dreams.

Look how the golden children
are climbing up the silver poplars to the sky!

And the blue of their lovely
eyes and the sky are touching . . . Eyes and sky are one!

Look how the golden children
are climbing the silver poplars to the sky!

JUAN RAMÓN JIMÉNEZ

CON LAS ROSAS

No, esta dulce tarde
no puedo quedarme;
esta tarde libre
tengo que irme al aire.

Al aire que ríe
abriendo los árboles,
amores a miles,
profundo, ondeante.

Me esperan las rosas
bañando su carne.
¡No me claves fines;
no quiero quedarme!

JUAN RAMÓN JIMÉNEZ

WITH THE ROSES

No, this sweet afternoon
I cannot stay indoors;
this free afternoon
I must go out in the open air.

Into the laughing air,
spreading through the trees
thousands of loves,
profound and waving.

The roses await me,
bathing their flesh.
No boundaries contain me;
I will not stay indoors.

JUAN RAMÓN JIMÉNEZ

PRIMAVERA AMARILLA

Abril venía, lleno
todo de flores amarillas:
amarillo el arroyo,
amarillo el vallado, la colma,
el cementerio de los niños,
el huerto aquel donde el amor vivía.

El sol unjía de amarillo el mundo,
con sus luces caídas;
¡ay, por los lirios áureos,
el agua de oro, tibia;
las amarillas mariposas
sobre las rosas amarillas!

Guirnaldas amarillas escalaban
los árboles; el día
era una gracia perfumada de oro,
en un dorado despertar de vida.
Entre los huesos de los muertos,
abría Dios sus manos amarillas.

JUAN RAMÓN JIMÉNEZ

YELLOW SPRING

April came, full
of yellow flowers.
The brook was yellow,
the stone walls were yellow, the hill,
the children's graveyard,
and the orchard where love was living.

The sun anointed the world with yellow,
with downpouring rays;
ah, through the golden lilies,
the warm golden water,
the yellow butterflies
over the golden roses.

Yellow garlands were climbing
up the trees, the day
was a grace perfumed with gold
in a golden awakening of life.
Among the bones of the dead,
God opened his yellow hands.

JUAN RAMÓN JIMÉNEZ

21

LA PLAZA Y LOS NARANJOS ENCENDIDOS . . .

La plaza y los naranjos encendidos
con sus frutas redondas y risueñas.

Tumulto de pequeños colegiales
que, al salir en desorden de la escuela,
llenan el aire de la plaza en sombra
con la algazara de sus voces nuevas.

¡Alegría infantil en los rincones
de las ciudades muertas! . . .
¡Y algo nuestro de ayer, que todavía
vemos vagar por estas calles viejas!

ANTONIO MACHADO

THE PLAZA AND THE FLAMING ORANGE TREES . . .

The plaza and the flaming orange trees
with their round and smiling fruit.

Clamor of small schoolchildren
scampering wildly out of school,
filling the air of the somber plaza
with the tumult of their new voices.

Childish cheer on the corners
of the dead towns! . . .
And something out of our yesterday, still
lingering in these old streets!

ANTONIO MACHADO

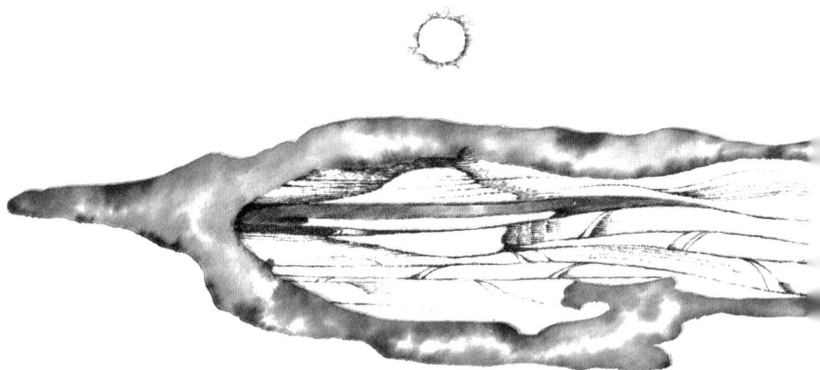

CANCION TONTA

Mamá.
Yo quiero ser de plata.

Hijo,
tendrás mucho frío.

Mamá.
Yo quiero ser de agua.

Hijo,
tendrás mucho frío.

Mamá.
Bórdame en tu almohada.

¡Eso sí!
¡Ahora mismo!

FEDERICO GARCÍA LORCA

SILLY SONG

Mama.
I wish I were silver.

Son,
you'd be very cold.

Mama.
I wish I were water.

Son,
you'd be very cold.

Mama.
Embroider me on your pillow.

That, yes!
Right away!

FEDERICO GARCÍA LORCA

CARACOLA

Me han traído una caracola.

Dentro le canta
un mar de mapa.
Mi corazón
se llena de agua,
con pececillos
de sombra y plata.

Me han traído una caracola.

FEDERICO GARCÍA LORCA

SNAIL

They have brought me a snail.

Inside it sings
a map-green ocean.
My heart
swells with water,
with small fish
of brown and silver.

They have brought me a snail.

FEDERICO GARCÍA LORCA

EL NIÑO MUDO

El niño busca su voz.
(La tenía el rey de los grillos.)
En una gota de agua
buscaba su voz el niño.

No la quiero para hablar;
me haré con ella un anillo
que llevará mi silencio
en su dedo pequeñito.

En una gota de agua
buscaba su voz el niño.

(La voz cautiva, a lo lejos,
se ponía un traje de grillo.)

FEDERICO GARCÍA LORCA

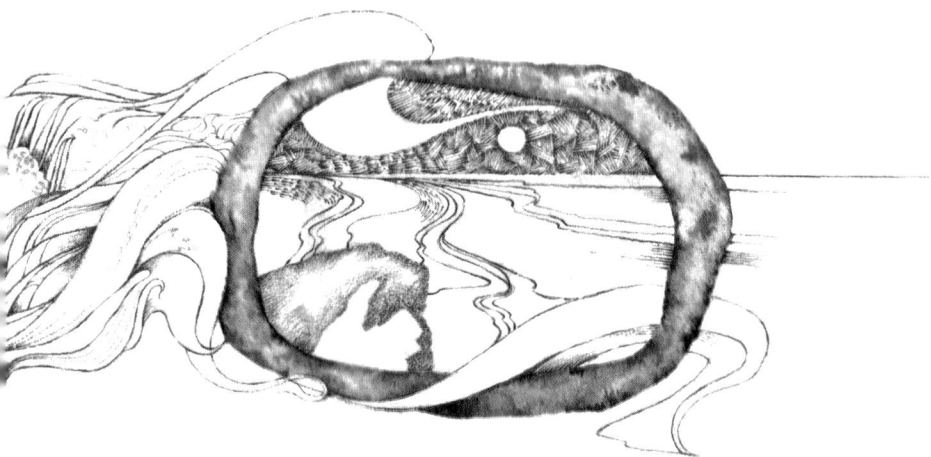

THE LITTLE MUTE BOY

The little boy was looking for his voice.
(The king of the crickets had it.)
In a drop of water
the little boy was looking for his voice.

I do not want it for speaking with;
I will make a ring of it
so that he may wear my silence
on his little finger.

In a drop of water
the little boy was looking for his voice.

(The captive voice, far away,
put on a cricket's clothes.)

FEDERICO GARCÍA LORCA

EL LAGARTO ESTA LLORANDO . . .

El lagarto está llorando.
La lagarta está llorando.

El lagarto y la lagarta
con delantaritos blancos.

Han perdido sin querer
su anillo de desposados.

¡Ay, su anillito de plomo,
ay, su anillito plomado!

Un cielo grande y sin gente
monta en su globo a los pájaros.

El sol, capitán redondo,
lleva un chaleco de raso.

¡Miradlos qué viejos son!
¡Qué viejos son los lagartos!

¡Ay, cómo lloran y lloran,
¡ay! ¡ay! cómo están llorando!

FEDERICO GARCÍA LORCA

PAUSE OF THE CLOCK

I sat down
in a space of time.
It was a backwater
of silence,
a white silence,
a formidable ring
wherein the stars
collided with the twelve floating
black numerals.

FEDERICO GARCÍA LORCA

BESIDE THE SIERRA IN FLOWER

Beside the sierra in flower
the broad sea bubbles.
In my honeycomb of bees
are small grains of salt.

ANTONIO MACHADO

EL SOL ES UN GLOBO DE FUEGO

El sol es un globo de fuego,
la luna es un disco morado.

Una blanca paloma se posa
en el alto ciprés centenario.

Los cuadros de mirtos parecen
de marchito velludo empolvado.

¡El jardín y la tarde tranquila! . . .
Suena el agua en la fuente de mármol.

ANTONIO MACHADO

THE SUN IS A GLOBE OF FIRE

The sun is a globe of fire,
the moon a purple disk.

A white dove perches
in a high centennial cypress.

The borders of myrtle
are like faded, dusty velvet.

Garden and quiet afternoon! . . .
Water drips in the marble fountain.

ANTONIO MACHADO

AGOSTO

Agosto,
contraponientes
de melocotón y azúcar,
y el sol dentro de la tarde,
como el hueso de una fruta.
La panocha guarda intacta,
su risa amarilla y dura.
Agosto.
Los niños comen
pan moreno y rica luna.

FEDERICO GARCÍA LORCA

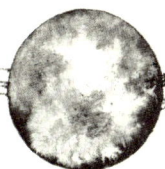

AUGUST

August,
counterpoints
of sugar and peach,
and the sun within the afternoon
like a fruit's core.
   The ear of grain keeps intact
its hard yellow laughter.
   August.
Children eat
brown bread and delicious moon.

FEDERICO GARCÍA LORCA

CASIDA DE LA MUCHACHA DORADA

La muchacha dorada
se bañaba en el agua
y el agua se doraba.

Las algas y las ramas
en sombra la asombraban,
y el ruiseñor cantaba
por la muchacha blanca.

Vino la noche clara
turbia de plata mala,
con peladas montañas
bajo la brisa parda.

La muchacha mojada
era blanca en el agua
y el agua, llamarada.

Vino el alba sin mancha,
con mil caras de vaca,
yerta y amortajada
con heladas guirnaldas.

La muchacha de lágrimas
se bañaba entre llamas,
y el ruiseñor lloraba
con alas quemadas.

La muchacha dorada
era una blanca garza
y el agua la doraba.

FEDERICO GARCÍA LORCA

CASIDA OF THE GOLDEN GIRL

The golden girl
bathed in the water
and the water turned golden.

The algae and the branches
in shadow shadowed her,
and the nightingale sang
for the white girl.

The clear night came
muddied with evil silver,
with bare mountains
under the tawny breeze.

The wet girl
was white in the water,
and the water ablaze.

The unblemished dawn came
with its thousand cow faces,
stiff and shrouded
with frozen garlands.

The girl of tears
bathed among flames,
and the nightingale wept
with charred wings.

The golden girl
was a white heron
and the water gilded her.

FEDERICO GARCÍA LORCA

¡*V*erdes jardinillos,
claras plazoletas,
fuente verdinosa
donde el agua sueña,
donde el agua muda
resbala en la piedra! . . .

Las hojas de un verde
mustio, casi negras,
de la acacia, el viento
de septiembre besa,
y se lleva algunas
amarillas, secas,
jugando, entre el polvo
blanco· de la tierra.

Linda doncellita
que el cántaro llenas
de agua transparente,
tú, al verme, no llevas
a los negros bucles
de tu cabellera,
distraídamente,
la mano morena,
ni, luego, en el limpio
cristal te contemplas . . .

Tú miras al aire
de la tarde bella,
mientras de agua clara
el cántaro llenas.

ANTONIO MACHADO

Green little gardens,
bright little squares,
verdigris fountain,
where water dreams,
where mute water
slips over stone! . . .

Leaves of faded
green, almost black,
of the acacias—the wind
of September has
stripped their flowers
and carried a few,
yellow and dry,
to play there in the white
dust of the earth.

Pretty girl,
filling your pitcher
with transparent water,
when you catch sight of me you don't
lift your brown hand
and arrange the black curls
of your hair
and admire yourself
in the limpid crystal . . .

You gaze into the air
of the beautiful evening
while the clear water
fills your pitcher.

ANTONIO MACHADO

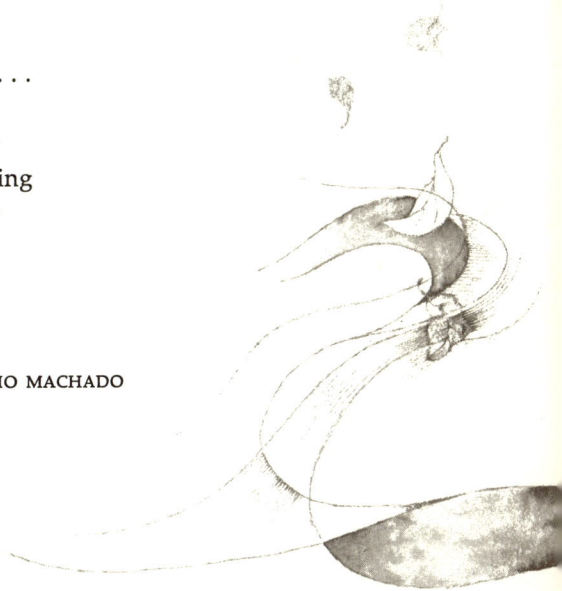

BALCON

La Lola
canta saetas.
Los toreritos
la rodean,
y el barberillo
desde su puerta,
sigue los ritmos
con la cabeza.
Entre la albahaca
y la hierbabuena,
la Lola canta
saetas.
La Lola aquella,
que se miraba
tanto en la alberca.

FEDERICO GARCÍA LORCA

BALCONY

Lola
sings *saetas*.
The little bullfighters
circle around her,
and the little barber,
from his doorway,
follows the rhythms
with his head.
Between the sweet basil
and the mint,
Lola sings
saetas.
That same Lola
who looked so long
at herself in the pool.

FEDERICO GARCÍA LORCA

SOÑE QUE TU ME LLEVABAS

Soñé que tú me llevabas
por una blanca vereda,
en medio del campo verde,
hacia el azul de las sierras,
hacia los montes azules,
una mañana serena.

Sentí tu mano en la mía,
tu mano de compañera,
tu voz de niña en mi oído
como una campana nueva,
como una campana virgen
de un alba de primavera.
¡Eran tu voz y tu mano,
en sueños, tan verdaderas!...
Vive, esperanza, ¡quién sabe
lo que se traga la tierra!

ANTONIO MACHADO

I DREAMED YOU LED ME

I dreamed you led me
along a white footpath
through green fields,
toward the blue of the sierras,
toward the blue mountains,
one serene morning.

I felt your hand in mine,
your companion hand,
your child's voice in my ear
like a new bell,
the pristine bell
of a spring dawn.
It was your voice and hand
in dreams, so true! . . .
Live, hope, who knows
what the earth devours!

ANTONIO MACHADO

VARIACION

El remanso del aire
bajo la rama del eco.

El remanso del agua
bajo fronda de luceros.

El remanso de tu boca
bajo espesura de besos.

FEDERICO GARCÍA LORCA

CANCION

Arriba canta el pájaro,
y abajo canta el agua.
—Arriba y abajo,
se me abre el alma—.

Mece a la estrella el pájaro,
a la flor mece el agua.
—Arriba y abajo,
me tiembla el alma—.

JUAN RAMÓN JIMÉNEZ

VARIATIONS

The still waters of the air
under the bough of the echo.

The still waters of the water
under a frond of stars.

The still waters of your mouth
under a thicket of kisses.

FEDERICO GARCÍA LORCA

SONG

Above the bird is singing,
and the water sings below.
—Above and below,
my soul is breaking—.

The bird is rocking the star,
and the water rocks the flower.
—Above and below,
my soul trembles—.

JUAN RAMÓN JIMÉNEZ

Por el monte ya llega
mi marido a comer.
El me trae una rosa
y yo le doy tres.

Por el llano ya vino
mi marido a cenar.
Las brasas que me entrega
cubro con arrayán.

Por el aire ya viene
mi marido a dormir.
Y alhelíes rojos
y él rojo alhelí.

Hay que juntar flor con flor
cuando el verano seca la sangre del segador.

FEDERICO GARCÍA LORCA

Los caminos de la tarde
se hacen uno, con la noche.
Por él he de ir a ti,
amor que tanto te escondes.

Por él he de ir a ti,
como la luz de los montes,
como la brisa del mar,
como el olor de las flores.

JUAN RAMÓN JIMÉNEZ

Down the mountain my husband
is coming to eat.
He brings me a rose
and I bring him three.

Through the fields
my husband came in to dine.
The hot coals he brings me
I cover with myrtle.

Through the night air my husband
is coming to sleep.
He like a gillyflower red
and I like red gillyflowers.

When summer saps the blood of the sower,
then let us join our flowers together.

FEDERICO GARCÍA LORCA

The afternoon roads
Become one at night.
By it I must go to you,
Love, so securely hidden.

By it I must go to you,
Like the light on the mountains,
Like the breeze from the sea,
Like the fragrance of flowers.

JUAN RAMÓN JIMÉNEZ

¡LAS FIGURAS DEL CAMPO SOBRE EL CIELO!

¡Las figuras del campo sobre el cielo!
Dos lentos bueyes aran
en un alcor, cuando el otoño empieza,
y entre las negras testas doblegadas
bajo el pesado yugo,
pende un cesto de juncos y retama,
que es la cuna de un niño;
y tras la yunta marcha
un hombre que se inclina hacia la tierra,
y una mujer que en las abiertas zanjas
arroja la semilla.
Bajo una nube de carmín y llama,
en el oro flúido y verdinoso
del poniente, las sombas se agigantan.

ANTONIO MACHADO

FIGURES IN THE FIELD AGAINST THE SKY!

Figures in the field against the sky!
Two slow oxen plowing
a knoll in early autumn:
between the black heads
bent below the heavy yoke
hangs a basket made of broom and reed—
a child's cradle.
Behind the team
a man plods, leaning toward the earth;
a woman
throws seed in open furrows.
Under a cloud of flame and crimson
in the green fluid gold of sunset,
these shadows grow gigantic.

ANTONIO MACHADO

EN MEDIO DE LA PLAZA Y SOBRE TOSCA PIEDRA

En medio de la plaza y sobre tosca piedra,
el agua brota y brota. En el cercano huerto
eleva, tras el muro ceñido por la hiedra,
alto ciprés la mancha de su ramaje yerto.

La tarde está cayendo frente a los caserones
de la ancha plaza, en sueños. Relucen las vidrieras
con ecos mortecinos de sol. En los balcones
hay formas que parecen confusas calaveras.

La calma es infinita en la desierta plaza,
donde pasea el alma su traza de alma en pena.
El agua brota y brota en la marmórea taza.
En todo el aire en sombra no más que el agua suena.

ANTONIO MACHADO

OVER COARSE ROCK IN THE MIDDLE OF THE SQUARE

Over coarse rock in the middle of the square,
water drips and drips. In the nearby grove a tall
cypress tree, behind an ivy-girded wall,
lifts a stain of rigid branches in the air.

The afternoon is falling into dreams, a lull
before the large houses in the plaza. Windows glare
with macabre echoes of the sun; forms stare
from balconies and fade like blurring skulls.

Across the barren plaza endless calm abounds
where the soul trails the outline of a tortured soul.
Water drips and drips in the marble bowl.
In all the air in shadow, only water sounds.

ANTONIO MACHADO

SEÑOR, YA ME ARRANCASTE LO QUE YO MAS QUERIA

Señor, ya me arrancaste lo que yo más quería.
Oye otra vez, Dios mío, mi corazón clamar.
Tu voluntad se hizo, Señor, contra la mía.
Señor, ya estamos solos mi corazón y el mar.

ANTONIO MACHADO

LORD, WHAT I MOST LOVED YOU TORE FROM ME

Lord, what I most loved you tore from me.
Hear again this heart cry out alone.
Your will was done, Lord, against my own.
Lord, now we are one, my heart and the sea.

ANTONIO MACHADO

CASIDA DEL LLANTO

He cerrado mi balcón
porque no quiero oir el llanto,
pero por detrás de los grises muros
no se oye otra cosa que el llanto.

Hay muy pocos ángeles que canten,
hay muy pocos perros que ladren,
mil violines caben en la palma de mi mano.

Pero el llanto es un perro inmenso,
el llanto es un ángel inmenso,
el llanto es un violín inmenso,
las lágrimas amordazan al viento,
y no se oye otra cosa que el llanto.

FEDERICO GARCÍA LORCA

FRIO NUEVO...

Frío nuevo: canta un gallo.
Trueno y luna: llora un niño.
Calle sola: se va un perro.
Aún anoche: piensa un hombre.

JUAN RAMÓN JIMÉNEZ

THE WEEPING

I have shut my windows.
I do not want to hear the weeping,
but from behind the gray walls,
nothing is heard but the weeping.

There are few angels that sing,
there are few dogs that bark,
a thousand violins fit in the palm of the hand.

But the weeping is an immense dog,
the weeping is an immense angel,
the weeping is an immense violin,
tears strangle the wind,
nothing is heard but the weeping.

FEDERICO GARCÍA LORCA

EARLY MORNING

New cold: cock crowing.
Thunder and moonlight: child weeping.
Lonely street: dog slinking.
Night still: man thinking.

JUAN RAMÓN JIMÉNEZ

AMANECER DE OTONO
A Julio Romero de Torres

Una larga carretera
entre grises peñascales,
y alguna humilde pradera
donde pacen negros toros. Zarzas, malezas, jarales.

Está la tierra mojada
por las gotas del rocío,
y la alameda dorada,
hacia la curva del río.

Tras los montes de violeta
quebrado el primer albor;
a la espalda la escopeta,
entre sus galgos agudos, caminando un cazador.

ANTONIO MACHADO

AUTUMN DAWNING

For Julio Romero de Torres

A long highway
between gray cliff sides,
and a lowly meadow
where black bulls graze. Blackberries, thickets, rockroses.

The earth is wet
with points of dew,
aspen rows are golden
near the river bend.

Behind the violet forests
first dawn is breaking;
on his shoulder a shotgun,
between his nimble hounds, a hunter walking.

ANTONIO MACHADO

CANCION DE INVIERNO

Cantan. Cantan.
¿Donde cantan los pájaros que cantan?

Ha llovido. Aún las ramas
están sin hojas nuevas. Cantan. Cantan
los pájaros. ¿En dónde cantan
los pájaros que cantan?

No tengo pájaros en jaulas.
No hay niños que los vendan. Cantan.
El valle está muy lejos. Nada. . .

Yo no sé dónde cantan
los pájaros—cantan, cantan—,
los pájaros que cantan.

JUAN RAMÓN JIMÉNEZ

WINTER SONG

Singing. Singing.
Where are the birds that are singing?

It has rained. And still the branches
have no new leaves Singing. Birds
are singing. Where are the birds
that are singing?

I have no birds in cages.
There are no children who sell them. Singing.
The valley is far away. Nothing. . .

I do not know where the birds are
that are singing—singing, singing—
the birds that are singing.

JUAN RAMÓN JIMÉNEZ

EN EL AZUL LA BANDA

En el azul la banda
de unos pájaros negros
que chillan, aletean y se posan
en el álamo yerto.
. . . En el desnudo álamo,
las graves chovas quietas y en silencio,
cual negras, frías notas
escritas en la pauta de febrero.

ANTONIO MACHADO

*A*nochecido, grandes nubes ahogan el pueblo.
Los faroles están tristes y soñolientos,
y la luna amarilla camina, entre agua y viento.

Viene un olor a campo mojado. Algún lucero
surje, verdoso, tras un campanario viejo.
El coche de las siete pasa. . . Ladran los perros. . .

Al salir al camino, se siente el rostro lleno
de luna fría. . . Sobre el blanco cementerio,
en la colina, lloran los altos pinos negros.

JUAN RAMÓN JIMÉNEZ

IN THE BLUE

In the blue
a band of black birds
that shriek, flutter, and alight
on a stiff poplar tree.
. . . In the naked grove
the grave quiet jackdaws
write cold black notes
on February staffs.

ANTONIO MACHADO

Nightfall. Large clouds smother the town.
The street lamps stand, drowsy and sorrowful,
and the yellow moon travels between rain and wind.

A moist odor ascends from the countryside.
A star rises, greenish, by the old spire.
The seven-o'clock stagecoach goes by . . . Dogs bark . . .

Coming out on the road, one feels upon his face
the cold moonlight . . . From the white cemetery,
upon the hill, comes the sobbing of the tall black pines.

JUAN RAMÓN JIMÉNEZ

MEDIA LUNA

La luna va por el agua.
¡Cómo está el cielo tranquilo!
Va segando lentamente
el temblor viejo del río
mientras que una rana joven
la toma por espejito.

FEDERICO GARCÍA LORCA

HALF MOON

The moon goes over the water.
How tranquil the sky is!
She goes scything slowly
the old shimmer from the river;
meanwhile a young frog
takes her for a little mirror.

FEDERICO GARCÍA LORCA

EL CONCIERTO INTERRUMPIDO

Ha roto la armonía
de la noche profunda,
el calderón helado y soñoliento
de la media luna.

Las acequias protestan sordamente
arropadas con juncias,
y las ranas, muecines de la sombra,
se han quedado mudas.

En la vieja taberna del poblado
cesó la triste música,
y ha puesto la sordina a su aristón
la estrella más antigua.

El viento se ha sentado en los torcales
de la montaña oscura,
y un chopo solitario—el Pitágoras
de la casta llanura—
quiere dar con su mano centenaria,
un cachete a la luna.

FEDERICO GARCÍA LORCA

THE INTERRUPTED CONCERT

The frozen sleepy pause
of the half moon
has broken the harmony
of the deep night.

The ditches, shrouded in sedge,
protest in silence,
and the frogs, muezzins of shadow,
have fallen silent.

In the old village inn
the sad music has ceased,
and the most ancient of stars
has muted its ray.

The wind has come to rest
in dark mountain caves,
and a solitary poplar—Pythagoras
of the pure plain—
lifts its aged hand
to strike at the moon.

FEDERICO GARCÍA LORCA

Cuando se abre en la mañana
roja como sangre está;
el rocío no la toca
porque se teme quemar.
Abierta en el mediodía
es dura como el coral,
el sol se asoma a los vidrios
para verla relumbrar.
Cuando en las ramas empiezan
los pájaros a cantar
y se desmaya la tarde
en las violetas del mar,
se pone blanca con blanco
de una mejilla de sal;
y cuando toca la noche
blando cuerno de metal
y las estrellas avanzan
mientras los aires se van,
en la raya de lo oscuro
se comienza a deshojar.

FEDERICO GARCÍA LORCA

In the morning unfolding,
red it is like blood.
Afraid of burning,
dew does not touch it.
At noon, it is wide open
and hard as coral.
Sun peeks though glass
to see it shine.
When birds in the branches
begin to sing,
and afternoon faints
in the violet tints of sea,
it turns white, white
as a cheek of salt;
and when night is struck
by a soft metallic horn,
and stars advance
as breezes go,
on the boundary line of darkness,
its petals begin to fall.

FEDERICO GARCÍA LORCA

El dormir es como un puente
que va del hoy al mañana.
Por debajo, como un sueño,
pasa el agua.

JUAN RAMÓN JIMÉNEZ

DESPEDIDA

Si muero,
dejad el balcón abierto.

El niño come naranjas.
(Desde mi balcón lo veo.)

El segador siega el trigo.
(Desde mi balcón lo siento.)

¡Si muero,
dejad el balcón abierto!

FEDERICO GARCÍA LORCA

Sleep is like a bridge
which reaches from today to tomorrow.
Below, like a dream,
the water flows by.

JUAN RAMÓN JIMÉNEZ

FAREWELL

If I die,
leave the balcony open.

The little boy is eating oranges.
(From my balcony I can see him.)

The reaper is harvesting the wheat.
(From my balcony I can hear him.)

If I die,
leave the balcony open!

FEDERICO GARCÍA LORCA

EL VIAJE DEFINITIVO

... Y yo me iré. Y se quedarán los pájaros
cantando;
y se quedará mi huerto, con su verde árbol,
y con su pozo blanco.

Todas las tardes, el cielo será azul y plácido;
y tocarán, como esta tarde están tocando,
las campanas del campanario.

Se morirán aquellos que me amaron;
y el pueblo se hará nuevo cada año;
y en el rincón aquel de mi huerto florido y encalado,
mi espíritu errará, nostálgico...

Y yo me iré; y estaré solo, sin hogar, sin árbol
verde, sin pozo blanco,
sin cielo azul y plácido...
Y se quedarán los pájaros cantando.

JUAN RAMÓN JIMÉNEZ

THE CONCLUSIVE VOYAGE

I shall go away. And the birds will still be there,
singing,
and my garden will be there with its green tree
and its white well.

Each afternoon the sky will be blue and peaceful,
and the notes will ring out as this afternoon they ring out
from the bells of the belltower.

And those who love me will be dead,
and the village will renew itself each year,
and in the corner of my flowering, whitewashed garden,
my spirits shall wander nostalgically . . .

And I shall go away; and be alone, homeless, with no
green tree, with no white well,
with no blue and peaceful sky,
and the birds will still be there, singing.

JUAN RAMÓN JIMÉNEZ

FEDERICO GARCIA LORCA was born in Fuenteva-
queros, Spain, in 1889. He studied in local schools and
at the University of Granada. In 1921 his first book of
poems was published. This book caught the attention
of Juan Ramón Jiménez, who invited Lorca to collabo-
rate with him in his literary magazine, *Indice*. The fol-
lowing year, 1922, Lorca, along with the famous Spanish
composer Manuel de Falla, organized a festival of folk
music and folk poetry in Granada.

Lorca came briefly to New York in 1929. Returning to
Spain he started a traveling theater company, "La Bar-
raca." It was during this period that Lorca wrote many
of his finest poetic dramas.

In 1936, the year of the outbreak of the Civil War in
Spain, Lorca was arrested and shot while visiting a
friend in Granada.

Born in 1881 in Moguer, *JUAN RAMON JIMENEZ* was educated in local Jesuit schools and eventually at the University of Seville. His poetry first began to attract attention when it was published in newspapers in Seville. In 1900, while in Madrid, Jiménez published his first two books of poetry. His famous prose work, *Platero and I*, in which the poet converses with his small donkey, was published in 1917, the same year he married Zenobia Camprubí. Jiménez and his wife began collaborating on many literary projects, one of the most ambitious being a translation into Spanish of the complete works of the Hindu poet Rabindranath Tagore.

During the Spanish Civil War, Jiménez came to Puerto Rico, and subsequently to the United States. Two years before he died in 1958, he was awarded the Nobel Prize for literature.

Born in Seville in 1875, *ANTONIO MACHADO* was the son of a jurist who was known for his outstanding work in Spanish folklore. Machado, who was educated in Madrid, immersed himself deeply in Castilian culture. After his studies, he worked for a while in Paris as a translator. He returned to Spain in 1907 where he taught French in a high school in Soria, and where in 1909 he married. Three years later, his young bride suddenly died—an event that had a strong influence on the poetry Machado wrote thereafter.

Machado spent the rest of his life as a schoolteacher, until the Civil War, in which he defended the cause of Loyalist Spain. Forced to flee his country, he died in France in 1939.

INDEX OF FIRST LINES (Spanish)

INDEX OF FIRST LINES (English)

SELECTED READING

About GARCIA LORCA:

R. Campbell: *Lorca*, England, Cambridge University Press, 1952.

E. Honig: *García Lorca*, New York, New Directions, 1944.

J. B. Trend: F. *García Lorca and the Spanish Poetic Tradition*, New York, Oxford University Press, 1945.

About JUAN RAMON JIMENEZ:

E. Florit: Preface, *The Selected Writings of Juan Ramón Jiménez*, New York, Grove Press, 1957.

J. B. Trend: *Juan Ramón Jiménez*, New York, Oxford University Press, 1950.

About ANTONIO MACHADO:

A. J. McVan: *Antonio Machado*, New York, Hispanic Society of America, 1959.

J. R. Jiménez: "A. Machado," *Antioch Review* 18 (1958) pp. 272-74.

J. B. Trend: *A. Machado*, New York, Oxford University Press, Dolphin Book Co., 1953.